You Are a Gift

Eraina Tinnin

You Are a Gift

A Teen Girl's Guide to Self-Discovery

Foreword By:
Laticia Nicole Beatty

Pearly Gates Publishing, LLC, Houston, Texas

You Are a Gift

You Are a Gift:
A Teen Girl's Guide to Self-Discovery

Copyright © 2017
Eraina Tinnin

All Rights Reserved.
No portion of this publication may be reproduced, stored in any electronic system, or transmitted in any form or by any means (electronic, mechanical, photocopy, recording, or otherwise) without written permission from the publisher. Brief quotations may be used in literary reviews.

Scripture references marked ESV and NIV are used with permission from Zondervan via Biblegateway.com

ISBN 13: 978-1-945117-94-7
Library of Congress Control Number: 2017957312

For information and bulk ordering, contact:
Pearly Gates Publishing, LLC
Angela Edwards, CEO
P.O. Box 62287, Houston, TX 77205
BestSeller@PearlyGatesPublishing.com

Dedication

This book is dedicated to my nieces,
Braylin Leahr and Blake Briggs.

I believe in you and I pray that you know
YOU are truly a
"GIFT"
to this world.

You Are a Gift

Acknowledgments

THANKING GOD for giving me the vision to write this book. If it were not for Him, the book probably would not have been written.

I thank my husband, **Corey**, for his support for the past 26 years. You have been my rock during everything. I appreciate you. The best is yet to come!

To my children, **Courtney and Jordan** — my two heartbeats: *THANK YOU*. You have supported me, encouraged me, and held me accountable. This is for **YOU**.

To **Angela Edwards of Pearly Gates Publishing** — the most *AMAZING* Publisher and Editor: I thank you for your patience and always being accessible to me, no matter the hour. You are a jewel. I am looking forward to working with you on future projects. ☺

Eraina Tinnin

To my parents, **Karen and Lee Briggs**: Thank you for your undying support and encouragement. They are what help me pursue my dreams and goals. Knowing that you have my back and that you support me are what keep me going. I pray I am making you proud.

To **Nakia P. Evans**: *THANK YOU* for being **YOU**. We've only known each other a year, but *OMG!* It's like we are one. We have so much in common and share some of the same goals and visions. It is refreshing to have a likeminded friend who understands business, passion, and destiny; a person who encourages and supports, and although our brands are similar, there is **NO COMPETITION**. I love you and am looking forward to making our *Beautiful You Authentic You* brand **internationally** known. We have work to do! 😊

You Are a Gift

To all the **parents** who purchase this book for their girls: ***THANK YOU!*** I pray it blesses them reading it as much as it did me writing it.

TABLE OF CONTENTS

Dedication vi

Acknowledgments.. vii

Foreword.. xi

Introduction xiii

Chapter 1 - I Love Me..1

Chapter 2 - Uniquely You 14

Chapter 3 - Forgive to Be Forgiven 25

Chapter 4 - Belief 36

Chapter 5 - Friendship..44

Chapter 6 - Fear No More 53

Chapter 7 - I Feel So Alone 63

Chapter 8 - Love Your Neighbor...............................71

Chapter 9 - Boys & Dating.......................................81

Chapter 10 - Just for Fun...90

Chapter 11 - Parents Just Don't Understand 98

Chapter 12 - Be Happy 107

Chapter 13 - Social Media 116

Words of Encouragement 125

Words from the Author 127

About the Author 130

Connect with Eraina Tinnin: 132

You Are a Gift

Foreword

You Are a Gift: A Teen Girl's Guide to Self-Discovery by Eraina Tinnin is a masterpiece that should be on the bookshelf of **every** teenage girl, church, library, and counselor.

Eraina Tinnin is an amazing 3-Time Best-Selling Author whom I've been able to work with co-authoring my very own book, *Healing Toxic Habits*. Eraina speaks from real-life stories that will impact the world — one person at a time. Her ability to connect with women **and** girls is amazing!

This book is powerful, and I, Laticia Nicole of Speak Life Enterprise, encourage **every** woman and girl to read **every** word. Allow the words to teach, guide, renew, and rebuke you. Allow yourself to be led down a road that has been mapped out by a woman who has traveled through life's ups and downs and made it through.

You can now avoid getting lost among the roadblocks and detours. **Enjoy!**

~ Laticia Nicole Beatty ~
#SpeakLife
www.LaticiaNicole.com

You Are a Gift

Introduction

The teen years are difficult years. I've lived through them and have raised a daughter who lived through them as well. They are the years where you fall in between being a little girl and an adult. You are neither, and being in that "middle space" can be quite difficult.

There are several questions you may ask yourself as you begin to find YOU:

Do I make my own decisions?

Do I only do what my parents say?

Are my friends really my friends?

Do I like what I see what I look in the mirror?

What does the future hold for me?

Am I smart enough?

Am I pretty enough?

Eraina Tinnin

Does he like me?

What am I going to do after high school?

Why does she keep picking on me?

These are the types of questions that may cross your mind as you transition into the next phase of life. You may feel as if your parents don't understand you. You may also feel as if you don't fit in with your friends. I mean, they are your friends but you are **different**; you think *different*, you have *different* ideas, *different* interests, dress *different*, and you might even look *different*. You think it's okay to be yourself...but is it really? Do people really accept you for who you truly are? Do **YOU** accept *YOU*?

You may feel as if you have nowhere to turn and no one to talk to. You may also feel as if you are the **ONLY** one who feels the way you do. You feel alone, confused, rejected, anxious, unloved, and worried.

You Are a Gift

Does any of this sound familiar?

This book is written with **YOU** in mind. It's a book that is created just for **YOU**. It is designed to encourage, inspire, and empower you. It is a book that will have scriptural references, guidance, and advice. It will have affirmations and activities to help you think and become a better *YOU*. It is a book meant to help you along the way as you begin the journey to **SELF-DISCOVERY.**

You, my dear, are not alone. God says in His Word that He will never leave you nor forsake you. Never means **NEVER**. No matter what obstacles come your way, He will always be right by your side.

It is important at this time in your life to realize who you are and what you were created to do. It is important at this stage in your life to not care what others think about you—

except *GOD*. It is important to realize that good things and bad things will happen in your life, and the bad things should help develop you, make you stronger, and build your character. You should not get stuck in the bad; **GROW** from it, **LEARN** from it, and move on.

It is important at this stage of your life to realize what a true friend is and to learn when someone is genuine...and when someone is not. You should also learn the following lesson: To **HAVE** a friend is to **BE** a friend. In other words, treat others the way you want to be treated.

It is important to learn that the choices you make have consequences. It is important to learn that you **WILL** make mistakes — and it's okay! It's a part of the learning process.

It is important to learn that you **ARE** special. You **ARE** important. You do *MATTER*.

YOU ARE A GIFT!

Chapter 1
I Love Me

"To acquire wisdom is to love oneself."
Proverbs 19:8 (NIV)

I love me. I love me. I love me. When you look in the mirror, do you like what you see? Do you have confidence? Do you always feel good about yourself? Do you love yourself? As a teenager, there may be times (often) when you don't like, let alone *LOVE*, yourself. This is a time in your life that is a transitional period. You are transitioning from a little girl to a teenager to a young woman. It takes time to grow into who you are to become and who God created you to be.

You will be unsure of a lot of things. You may lack confidence and self-love. You may even compare yourself to others. You may think girls are prettier than you and more athletic than you.

They get invited to all the parties and the boys like them.

What you have to realize is **YOU** are special, beautiful, smart, and loveable, too! God created you to be uniquely **YOU**. You were created to stand apart.

God says in 1st Peter 2:9, "*But you are a chosen people, a royal priesthood, a holy nation, God's special possession, that you may declare the praises of Him who called you out of darkness into His wonderful light*". That scripture means you are **CHOSEN**, **ROYAL**, **HOLY**, and **SPECIAL**!!! You may not *feel* any of those things about yourself but because **GOD** said it, it is true.

You may feel as if you aren't loved because it isn't shown by your parents, family, or friends. You don't feel love, so you don't love yourself; but **GOD** loves you! He *always* has and *always* will. In addition to loving you, He will **NEVER** leave nor forsake you. That means in spite of how you might feel, you are **NEVER ALONE**! How comforting is it to know that you will *NEVER* be alone? God knows each hair on your head and even knew you when you were formed in your mother's womb! **WHAT???** Do you realize how special you are? I'm sure **you** don't even know the number of hairs on your head, but God does! If He takes the time to *KNOW YOU*, then you should take the time to **KNOW HIM**. He created you—and everything He created is **GOOD**!

YES. That includes *YOU*!

It may be hard to believe that you are special—royalty, even—especially if you care what others think about you. There will be people your entire life who will not like you for *NO REASON AT ALL*. That may be hard to believe but it's true. Some may be jealous and want what you have *(even though you may want more)*. They may not have the family environment or the support you have. The may be without someone who loves them. They may even have a family but no quality time is spent doing 'family things'. No time is spent sharing how they are loved. No time is spent encouraging, inspiring, or empowering them to be the best they can be; *OR* that person could be **YOU**. When you don't have the love and support you need nor hear the words of affirmation, it could cause you to have low self-esteem.

What exactly is "*low self-esteem*"? Webster's Dictionary defines it as "…*a favorable impression of oneself*". Do you have a **FAVORABLE** impression of yourself? In my experience, the teen years are the years that you *DON'T* find yourself favorable. They are the years you compare yourself to others and are in the process of self-discovery, finding out exactly who you are and what you like. It is a time that you are learning **WHO YOU ARE**. You begin to have your own ideas, opinions, and

I Love Me

views about things—and **THAT'S OKAY**. You begin to question more and some may disagree with you. Based on the opinion or advice of others is when you start to either voice your own opinion or withdraw.

The teenage years are when you begin to seek answers to questions and try things that are good for you (and some that are not). The important thing that you must remember is that in the **PROCESS** of becoming who you are, *LOVE YOURSELF*—no matter what.

No matter what anyone says.

No matter what anyone thinks.

No matter what anyone does.

You are *LOVABLE* and deserve to be loved, **ESPECIALLY** by *YOU*. Hold yourself in the highest regard, no matter how different you are from those around you. You are different for a reason. God made you to **STAND OUT**.

Imagine if everyone was the same. Think of how boring the world would be. You were created with a purpose and for a purpose. The sooner you find out what that purpose is, the sooner you can begin to fulfill your destiny.

Bad things will happen to you. You are no different than anyone else. So, no matter how **GOOD** you are, *BAD* things will happen. What I want you to do is **LEARN** from the bad and **USE** it to do *GOOD*. Don't dwell on it. Don't stress about it. Don't allow it to consume you. "*It*" happened. "*It*" may happen again. However, "*it*" doesn't change the fact that you are special and unique. Think about it: Since God is for you, **WHO** can be against you? The answer to that is *NO ONE.*

I Love Me

You will lose friends — or people you think are your friends, you find really are not. You are discovering what it is to be a friend and to have one *(this is discussed later in the book)*. **LOVE YOURSELF** anyway. When your 'fake friends' hurt and betray you, *THANK GOD* you were able to see their true colors. Pray for God to bring you like-minded friends who have the same interests and do the same things you do. He will do it!

Eraina Tinnin

Personal Reflection

When I was a teenager, I didn't love myself. In all honesty, I probably didn't begin to truly love myself until I was in my 30s. That's a **LONG** time to not love myself. I had low self-esteem and cared *SO MUCH* about what other people thought of me. Although I was happy most of the time, there were times when I hid my sadness and didn't allow it to show.

When I began to believe what God said about me *(I am fearfully and wonderfully made; I am more than a conqueror; I can do **ALL** things through Christ who gives me strength; I am the head and not the tail; I am above and not beneath)* — when I actually began to first learn those things and then **BELIEVE** those things, I became unstoppable. I knew there was **NOTHING** I couldn't do!

I Love Me

What I am telling you is the things that you may be experiencing are because I **EXPERIENCED** them, too…and look at me *NOW!*

Affirmation

I love me.
I love me because God made me.
I love me because I am special.
I love me because I am unique.
I love me because I **DESERVE**
to be loved.

I Love Me

Activity

Write 20 — **YES, 20!** — things that you *LOVE* about yourself. Read them **EVERY DAY** until you start to *BELIEVE THEM*.

1. _____

2. _____

3. _____

4. _____

5. _____

6. _____

7. _____

_____

8. _____

_____

9. _____

_____

10. _____

_____

11. _____

_____

12. _____

_____

13. _____

_____

14. _____

_____

I Love Me

15. _____

_____

16. _____

_____

17. _____

_____

18. _____

_____

19. _____

_____

20. _____

_____

Chapter 2
Uniquely You

"However, you are a chosen people, a royal priesthood, a holy nation, people who belong to God"
1 Peter 2:9 (NIV)

You are unique. There is **NO ONE** in the world like you. Someone may have the same name as you or even have the same birthday. They may even resemble you and have similar interests but there is **NO ONE** in the ***ENTIRE*** world just like *YOU*. How does that make you feel? Does it make you feel special? Does it make you feel strange or weird? Think about the billions of people in the world and then realize there is only **ONE** you.

You are unique.

You are set apart.

Uniquely You

You are chosen.

You are royalty.

You have gifts and talents that **NO ONE** else has. Yes, others may be able to sing, draw, act, or dance—but they can't do it *JUST LIKE YOU*. It is impossible because there is no one else like you!

Because there is no one else like you, it could be challenging during this transitional period. You may want to walk in who you believe you are and who God called you to be. This could mean separating yourself from your "friends" because they don't understand. You may like to write instead of listening to music. You may prefer hanging out at a café rather than going to a concert. Maybe the clothes you like are different from other kids. You could even like crazy, bright hair colors (like orange or pink). Knowing that God made you this way should cause you to feel special. However, because of your differences, be prepared to be an outcast.

Remember: God said you were "chosen" and "set apart" in 1st Peter 2:9. It is expected that you are to **BE** different.

Your parents may not understand you. Your teachers may not understand you. Your friends and family may not understand you — and that is okay. God made **ALL** of us different. If everyone talked, walked, dressed, and looked the same, imagine how boring this world would be…

People may talk about you. They may laugh at you. They may make you feel uncomfortable; however, the sooner you realize that you are **ROYALTY** and a child of the *KING*, the better off you will be!

Because of your differences, people may even reject you. Have you already felt rejected?

Uniquely You

Do you feel like no one likes you or that you don't fit in? That is exactly what rejection is. Are there kids in your class who are constantly picked on for their differences?

Is that person **YOU**?

Whether it is you being rejected or someone else, it is **NOT** a good feeling. Everyone wants to feel accepted and liked. Make sure you aren't the one making others feel left out. At some point in life, everyone wants to feel included and a part of something. What if you were the one who was or is always an outcast — the one never invited to parties or who doesn't have the latest clothes (or really doesn't care what the latest styles are)? It is normal for you to be sad but don't allow it to take over your thoughts.

As a teenager, it may be hard for you to understand this but **GOD LOVES YOU**. He made you *UNIQUELY YOU*. Because of His love for you, you should never feel rejected. I know this is easy for me to say because I am not in your shoes; I am not a teenager (but I was at one time).

People will reject you. People will talk about you. People will leave you. People will hurt you.

GOD will do *NONE* of those things. You can count on Him to be a constant source of comfort **AND** support in your life, for the **REST** of your life. God made you who you are.

Don't change who you are for **ANYONE**. That includes family and friends. Dare to be different. Dare to be who **GOD** created you to be. Realize that people who don't accept you for who you are aren't your friends. *LOVE* covers a multitude (that means a lot) of sin. So, even if you are doing something people don't agree with or that you shouldn't do, their **LOVE** for you should not change.

Uniquely You

Be real. Be true. Be original. **BE YOU!**

Eraina Tinnin

Personal Reflection

Growing up, I hated my name. People always mispronounced it and misspelled it (sometimes, they *STILL* do). It got to the point where I stopped correcting people. Kids in school teased me because of my name. **I HATED IT!** Why couldn't I be named *Michelle* or *Kim* or *Stacy* — a name that was easy to pronounce **AND** easy to spell? Even now as an adult, people still don't take the time to learn to say my name correctly. If you look at my name, it's easy (to me) to say: Eraina *(E-Ray-Nah)*. I have been called Ariana, Araina, Iraina, Erania, Urania...and the list goes on.

When I went off to college, people still acted like they couldn't pronounce my name, so I told everyone, *"Just drop the "E" and call me 'Raina'"* — and that's what they did. So today, anyone who calls me Raina, I know we went to school together.

One day, one of my college classmates who happened to be from Panama said my name meant "Royalty". I told her "Thank you" but didn't really think much about it. Later, it dawned on me: **MY NAME MEANS ROYALTY!**

When I became an adult and married with children, people began to **COMPLIMENT** me on my name. *"Oh! That's so pretty!"* *"Oh! I like your name!"* When I began to see that my name was **UNIQUE, DIFFERENT**, and **SET APART**, that was when I truly began to *LOVE* my name. God made me **DIFFERENT** and gave me a *DIFFERENT* name to go along with my uniqueness.

Why would I want to be like anyone else? Why would I want a common name like everyone else? Why not embrace **MY NAME** and walk in my **_ROYALNESS_**? So, I did! I now *LOVE* my name. There aren't too many people in the world with my name. It's meant to be that way. I believe that God made me different. God made me unique. When I started believing that and believing what God said about me, I finally appreciated and embraced who I am.

Uniquely You

Affirmation

I am unique.
I am special.
I am royalty.

Activity

Write down five things that make you different from everyone else.

1. _____

   _____

2. _____

   _____

3. _____

   _____

4. _____

   _____

5. _____

   _____

Chapter 3
Forgive to Be Forgiven

"Be kind and compassionate to one another, forgiving each other, just as in Christ, God forgave you."
Ephesians 4:32 (NIV)

What does it mean to "*forgive*"? An example of forgiveness is if someone does something hurtful to you, lies on you, or steals from you, and although it hurt you, you manage to let it go and move on. It doesn't mean that you forget what they have done; it means you don't allow it to make you mean and bitter. When you see the person, you don't get an attitude and start thinking about how they hurt you.

We are all human. We all make mistakes. We may not do mean and bad things on purpose but we may end up hurting someone with our words or actions. God knows that we will make mistakes. There is no perfect person — except His Son, Jesus. God gave us rules to live by called 'Commandments'. We are to abide by the **10 Commandments.**

Your parents have also given you rules to live by. You may have a curfew and have to be home at a certain time. You may have to do chores before you can go and hang out with your friends. There may be some TV shows you aren't allowed to watch. There may be music you aren't allowed to listen to. There may be friends you aren't allowed to hang out with.

As a part of human nature, when someone tells us that we can't do something, we want to do it more. So, you may sneak and watch the shows you aren't supposed to watch, listen to the music you aren't supposed to listen to, and hang out with the friends you aren't supposed to. At some point in time, your parents may find out that you disobeyed them. They will be upset and disappointed but they will not hold it against you for the rest of your life. When we do something that requires forgiveness, God **WILL** forgive us — no matter *HOW MANY* times we ask Him to do so. And just like God forgives us, **WE** should also forgive others.

Let's say someone you called a 'friend' spread a rumor about you to everyone at school. Although you thought the person was your friend, they secretly didn't like you and got close to you to find out information they can share with others. If this happened, I am sure you would be devastated and hurt. You probably wouldn't want anything more to do with that person. If you find yourself in that position, you still *HAVE TO FORGIVE* them. Now, once that person showed you who they were, you no longer have to be friends (not that you were really friends in the first place) but you can still forgive them and move on. Will it be easy? **No.** Is it possible? **Yes!**

When you don't forgive, you have bitterness and anger in your heart. While you are walking around mad and upset, the person you are upset with is living life to the fullest. They are happy and don't have a care in the world. It's not worth it. When people show you who they are, believe them. Your 'friend' showed you that she didn't like you and couldn't be trusted. **BELIEVE** what she showed you. Forgive her — and love her from afar.

You may ask, "*How do I forgive?*" Forgiveness is something that is difficult to do, and you may not know exactly how to do it. Here are three tips that may help:

Forgive to Be Forgiven

1. ***Reach out to connect:*** You may have to reach out to the person who hurt you to initiate a conversation. They may not be open to it but you did your part by reaching out.
2. ***Ask them to listen:*** Even though you were the one hurt, ask them if they will listen and then tell them how you feel — what you thought of your friendship and how you felt after they hurt you. Before having that conversation, writing down your thoughts may help.
3. ***Discuss the issue:*** Have a conversation where both of you talk and share your feelings. Maybe they can share why they did what they did and you can share how it made you feel.

These steps can help you on the road to forgiveness. The steps will help you to forgive and move on. Even after you talk to the person, your friendship may never be the same. At least you had the chance to talk about it and (hopefully) resolve any issues.

Remember: If God can forgive you—no matter *HOW MANY* times you mess up—it is expected that you do the same.

Forgive to Be Forgiven

Personal Reflection

I remember when I was in high school, I had a very close friend. We spent a lot of time together. We went to the same school and always hung out together after school. We hung out on the weekends, too. She didn't have many friends, so I was one of her only friends. We did a lot together and were very close.

One day after school, a guy asked if he could give her a ride home. Typically, we rode the city bus together, as our school was downtown. She got into the car with him and left me there. That day, I ended up riding the bus home by myself.

I did not talk to my friend after that because I was hurt that she left me. She didn't even ask if he could give me a ride, too! I held a grudge against her for **YEARS** and did not talk to her again until we were both grown and married with children.

Looking back, it really showed my immaturity. We were great friends at the time…and we were young.

When we reconnected as adults, she didn't even remember the reason we stopped being friends. Eventually, I forgave her but my unforgiveness cost me a good friend.

Affirmation

I will forgive as I have been forgiven.

Activity

Think about a time someone hurt you. Write down how it made you feel and why it made you feel that way. Share here how you would feel if someone didn't forgive you.

_____

_____

_____

_____

_____

_____

_____

_____

_____

Forgive to Be Forgiven

Chapter 4
Belief

"Everything is possible for one who believes."
Mark 9:23 (NIV)

What does it mean to *"believe"*? Webster's Dictionary defines 'belief' as *"confidence, faith, and trust"*. During the transitional teen years, having confidence and belief in yourself may be difficult. You go through so many things and experience so much, you may find it hard to believe in yourself.

Maybe you tried out for cheerleading or the dance team but didn't make it. Maybe you were in a Spelling Bee and didn't win. Perhaps you are on a sports team but never get to play. It seems like every time you try out for something, you never make it.

Belief

You wanted to act and went to try out but got cut.

You wanted to dance but never get chosen as the lead.

Every job you applied for you didn't get.

You begin to doubt yourself and your abilities. You may not have anyone to encourage you to believe in yourself and to not give up. It is very important that you always believe in **YOU**. What if no one else does?

Belief begins in the mind. Whatever you think is what becomes. If you are always thinking negatively and saying negative things, negativity is what will consume you. You have to think and say positive things. That is why it is important to surround yourself with positive people, spend time with God, and read His Word. They say what goes in you is what comes out. So, if you put positivity and belief in, that is what will come out!

Belief is all about mindset. If your mind believes it, then you can achieve it. If you can think positive things, positive things will happen. I believe the reason we don't get what we want sometimes is because even though we want it, it isn't in God's plan for us; He has something bigger and better. So, maybe you didn't make the team or get that job: God has something bigger and better for you! You just have to ***BELIEVE*** it!

What is it that you don't believe can happen to and for you? What is the cause of your unbelief? Is it multiple letdowns? Is it disappointment from people? The scripture for this chapter says **ANYTHING** is possible — if you just *believe*. That means just what is says: You have to believe! Believe in yourself and your abilities.

Sometimes, you may not get the pat on the back or the encouragement you need. Sometimes,

Belief

you have to depend on **YOU** for encouragement and the support you need.

Believing in yourself starts with believing what God says about you. When you want to know how something works, you read the Instruction Manual. Well, God created us; so, when we want to know how **WE** work, we look in the Instruction Manual He gave us, which is the Bible. In the Bible, it says, *"We can do ALL things through Christ who gives us strength"* (Philippians 4:13, NIV). It also says, *"We are more than conquerors"* (Romans 8:37, NIV) and *"Anything is possible if we just believe"* (Mark 9:23, NIV). When you begin to read what God says **AND** believe what He says, things start to change. If God believes in you, why can't you believe in you? God doesn't make mistakes and He doesn't lie. What He says **IS**! You are everything you desire to be: smart, talented, and beautiful. Believe it, and it is so!

Eraina Tinnin

Personal Reflection

I didn't start believing in myself until I was an adult. This is part of the reason I want **YOU** to start believing in you *NOW* (if you don't already). Imagine growing up, having doubt about your abilities, and suffering from low self-esteem or lack of self-confidence. That was me.

I remember anytime I had to do something that required trying out for it, I **KNEW** or felt I wouldn't make it. I already set myself up to fail without even trying. I didn't believe in myself. I didn't have self-confidence and it caused me to place limits on *ME*. It wasn't until I began (as an adult) to read and believe the Word of God that I began to believe in *ME*. If God said something about me, why didn't I believe it? If He believed in me, then I **SHOULD** believe in *ME*, too!

There will be people who make you feel as if you can't do something and who won't believe

Belief

in you. **EXPECT** it. Even people who you think will be in your corner won't be there. As long as **YOU** believe in *YOU* and you know that God has your back, you will be okay.

It wasn't' until I believed what God said that I didn't care what other people said or thought about me. It no longer mattered what anyone said. All that mattered was what **GOD** said. His Word was *ALL* I needed.

Eraina Tinnin

Affirmation

I believe in **ME**.

Belief

Activity

Do something you have been meaning to do but haven't done because you didn't believe you could. It could be trying out for a sports team at school, running for student council, or applying for a job. **BELIEVE** that you will get it. *GIVE* it your all. Do the *BEST* you can. If, by chance, you **don't** get it, **BELIEVE** it wasn't for you. **KNOW** there is something out there that has ***ONLY YOUR NAME*** on it.

Chapter 5
Friendship

"A friend loves at all times."
Proverbs 17:17 (NIV)

Friendship is an important part of the teen years. Hopefully, you have some good friends you are able to create great memories with. As you grow and mature, your friends may change—and that's okay. You may develop different interests and grow in different directions—and that's okay. It is very important to have friends whom you can trust, share experiences with, and create pleasant memories with.

The teen years are tough. You may have people who you think are your friends but later realize they aren't. Maybe you aren't sure what

Friendship

a true friend is. Let me share with you the characteristics of a true friend:

A true friend is someone you can trust. You shouldn't have to worry that something you tell will be repeated. A true friend will celebrate good things with you (new job, making a team, scholarship, etc.). A true friend will support and encourage you if you want to try something new. A true friend will laugh and cry with you. A true friend will speak **TRUTH** to you—even if it hurts—because they have your best interest at heart. When you have a true friend, you enjoy spending time together and have similar interests. You can talk all day or you can sit and say nothing *(called 'comfortable silence')*. You are able to totally be yourself, no matter how strange or weird others may say you are. A true friend appreciates your differences. They will check on you if they haven't heard from you in a while, making sure you are alright. If you have a disagreement with each other, you talk about it and work through it; you don't go talking about each other to someone else.

People think they have to have a lot of friends. **BUT** if you have one or two *TRUE* friends, you are **BLESSED**! Also, keep in mind that as you grow and mature, you may grow apart from your friends — and that's okay. In my experience, God always brings just what you need when you need it.

Let's talk about what a friend is **NOT**:

A friend is not someone who shares all of your business. They will not gossip about you. A friend will not try to get you to do something you aren't comfortable doing **OR** ask you to do something that's not good for you (drugs, alcohol, sex, etc.). They won't pressure you or make fun of you in front of others. They don't act different

Friendship

around you when they are with their other friends. They never make you feel like an outcast.

With all of that said, to have a friend is to be a friend. So, if it is friendship you want, you have to make sure you are a friend in return. You can't go around being negative, causing drama, always frowning and complaining, and then expect to have a friendship.

To **HAVE** a friend, you must *BE* a friend.

Eraina Tinnin

__Personal Reflection__

God has truly blessed me with good friends. I am still friends with people I met back in middle school. My best friend (who I met in the 8th grade) was my friend all the way until we graduated and attended our first year of college. We ended up growing apart when I went off to college in a different state.

BUT...

We had our first three jobs together. We transferred high schools during our senior year and dressed alike that first week. We had so much in common and created so many memories. She is now married with three children and living on a different coast. Even though we don't talk much, I do know how to get in contact with her.

The relationship with my best friend in college was the same way. We were inseparable.

Friendship

People called us 'Two Bookends' because we were together so much. I even went to her hometown in a different state and spend Spring Break with her. We also went to another friend's house for Thanksgiving one year. We grew apart as well; however, if I need to reach her, I know how.

I have some very good friends now. I have friends I can count on — friends who are with me through the good and bad. Friends I can truly be myself with, and they love me still.

Growing up, I thought I had to have *ONE* best friend but as I have grown, I realized I can have the best in many friends — and that is exactly what I have.

Eraina Tinnin

Affirmation

I will be a good friend so that I can have a good friend.

Friendship

Activity

Describe what you believe are characteristics of a true friend. Look at your circle of friends and see who has *SHOWN* you (by their actions) that they are true friends. Ask yourself: **Would you want to be friends with you?**

_____

_____

_____

_____

_____

_____

_____

_____

_____

Chapter 6
Fear No More

"Have I not commanded you? Be strong and courageous. Do not be afraid; do not be discouraged, for the LORD your God will be with you wherever you go."
Joshua 1:9 (NIV)

Fear is something that limits a lot of people. You can be afraid of a thing (like a spider or snake) or the thought of something (like public speaking or swimming). When you actually think about fear, what exactly are you afraid of? If you are afraid of a spider, think about it like this: You are bigger than the spider, so what can it do to you?

In actuality, we aren't afraid of what we think we fear. If you are afraid of heights, you are really afraid of falling. If you are afraid of water, it's more than likely you have a fear of drowning more than the water itself.

God didn't give us the spirit of fear. In the above scripture, God instructs us to be strong and courageous, not afraid and discouraged. Fear can keep us from doing things we really want to do. It holds us hostage. Have you ever heard the saying, "***FEAR** is **F**alse **E**vidence **A**ppearing **R**eal*"? If so, that means it's **FALSE**—meaning you are afraid of something that isn't even real! How can you be afraid of something that isn't real?

I began to look at fear in a different light. It has changed my whole perspective. Instead of it being '*False Evidence Appearing Real*', it is now "***F**ace **E**verything **A**nd **R**ise*"! That means no matter what I am afraid of, instead of being fearful, I will **FACE** it. I will conquer it. I will master it—and **I WILL RISE**! I will not allow fear to hold me back.

Fear No More

I remember talking to a lady one day, and at the time, my daughter was about to go off to college. She was going to New York, which was miles and miles away from where we lived. The lady told me she was excited for my daughter and very proud of her. She also shared that she wanted to go off to New York to college years ago after graduating high school but she was *AFRAID* — afraid of being that far from home and going to a new city and state. As an adult, she admitted she **REGRETTED** not going.

Don't allow fear to hold you back from doing what you want to do. Think about it: If you actually did what you were afraid of, **WHAT** would happen? Would you still be living and breathing? Would the world end? I don't think so. So, instead of living life with regret, **GO AFTER** what you want. Do it with confidence and pride! Be *STRONG* and, as the scripture above says, be *COURAGEOUS*. Don't allow any negative, limited thinking **OR PEOPLE** hold you back from what *YOU* want to do. After all, it is **YOUR** life…and you only get one chance. **<u>ONLY ONE.</u>** You don't want to look back and wonder what could have, should have, and would have happened.

Fear No More

Personal Reflection

I used to allow fear to control me. I was afraid of walking in front of crowds of people. I even walked with my head down. I was afraid of speaking publicly. I was afraid of what people thought about me. I was a big ball of **FEAR**! 😊

I remember being in high school my senior year, and in my Social Studies class, we had to do a book report every quarter. In addition to the written report, we also had to do an oral report. I was terrified of getting in front of the class to speak. Just the *THOUGHT* of all my classmates looking at me terrified me. So, for three of the quarters, I didn't do the oral portion of the report. Finally, one of my best friends encouraged me to do it. It was the LAST quarter of the school year. Guess what? **I DID IT!** The whole time, I was nervous, my legs and voice were shaking, and I would not make eye contact with anyone. Still, I made it through! It was **VERY HARD** but *I DID IT!* I ended up getting a 98 on that report. **WOW!** Imagine if I had presented every quarter! When I went off to college, I **HAD** to take a speech class in order to graduate. *Go figure!*

When I started believing in God's Word, I began to overcome fear. Now, when I tell people I used to suffer from fear, it's hard for them to believe!

GOD SAYS I am more than a conqueror.

GOD SAYS I can do ALL things through Christ who gives me strength.

GOD SAYS He will never leave nor forsake me.

When I read what God said about me and believed it, I was able to overcome fear. It wasn't easy. It was a process — but I was able to do it, and you can, too!

Eraina Tinnin

Affirmation

I will not allow fear
to control me.

Activity

Make a list of things you are afraid of. Write down why you think you are afraid of them. List what you think would happen if you conquered your fears.

I encourage you to face one of your fears and write down how it felt after doing so.

_____

_____

_____

_____

_____

_____

_____

_____

_____

Chapter 7
I Feel So Alone

"Be strong and courageous. Do not be afraid or terrified because of them, for the LORD your God goes with you; He will never leave you nor forsake you."
Deuteronomy 31:6 (NIV)

Being or feeling alone is not a good feeling. You can even feel alone in a room full of people. Have you ever experienced that? Have you ever felt alone? What caused you to feel alone?

There are times you may feel like you have no one to turn to. You may have something you are going through and don't feel comfortable sharing with anyone. Even though your parents have always been supportive and you know you could talk to them, you choose not to or don't feel comfortable. You also don't feel like you can talk to your friends or any other family members. You may know the reason—or maybe you don't. All you know for sure is that you feel like you have no one. You have no one to turn to and you feel *ALL ALONE*.

When you feel alone, it can cause depression. Have you ever been depressed? It's not a good feeling, is it? It's kind of like being lonely. There is a bright side, though! God says He will **NEVER** leave nor forsake you! Never means ***NEVER***. That means whenever you feel like you are alone, you **ALWAYS** have *SOMEONE*. God is **ALWAYS** with you, no matter what. How comforting is that? Those times when you feel like you can't share what's going on with you or how you're feeling, you can **ALWAYS** share with God. He is, after all, your Heavenly Father. He already knows what you are going through. He just wants you to come to Him.

I Feel So Alone

I repeat: ***HE ALREADY KNOWS***. Nothing you go through is a surprise or secret to God. If nothing else, *THAT* should make you feel good. You should feel good knowing that you are **NEVER** alone.

NEVER alone.

NEVER alone.

NEVER ALONE!

Depression is something that can be a result of feeling alone. You become very sad and withdrawn. You want to isolate yourself from people and you sink deeper and deeper into a depression. In addition to talking to God, you can also write out your thoughts and feelings. Sometimes, *JUST GETTING IT OUT* helps. When you keep things bottled up, you can make yourself physically sick. You can begin to get headaches and even stomachaches. The **BEST** thing to do is surround yourself with positive people you can trust **AND** read God's Word. God's Word is a comfort and peace. You *WILL* feel uplifted and encouraged.

I Feel So Alone

Personal Reflection

Loneliness is something that everyone may experience at some point in time. Sometimes, you can feel lonely when you are in a room full of people. I have felt lonely on several occasions and even suffered from depression when I was in my 20s. I withdrew from people and felt all alone. I would just lie in my room and cry. It lasted a few days and then I would be up like nothing happened.

Looking back, I wish I had talked to someone so that I wouldn't have felt alone. **NO ONE** should go or feel as if they are going through things alone. I didn't grow up in church, so at that age, I knew who God was but didn't really have a relationship with Him or know what He said in His Word.

I am thankful now that I know God's Word. I know that if I ever feel alone or lonely,

HE IS THERE. *HE IS THERE ALWAYS AND FOREVER.* This brings me a sense of comfort and peace.

I Feel So Alone

Affirmation

I believe that God will **never** leave nor forsake me.

Eraina Tinnin

Activity

If you don't currently have one, go purchase a journal. You should write in it **EVERY** day. Share both your good and bad days on the pages of your journal. Write how you are feeling and what's going on with you.

Start out writing just five minutes a day and gradually increase if you need to. The purpose is to get your thoughts out and not have them bottled up. You can even address your entries to your *Daddy* (Heavenly Father, God); doing so will help you spend time with Him.

Chapter 8
Love Your Neighbor

"The second is this: 'Love your neighbor as yourself.'
There is no commandment greater than these."
Mark 12:31 (NIV)

Bullying is something that has been going on for a very long time. I think as time progresses, bullying gets worse. When I was growing up, bullying consisted of being picked on and teased. In this day and age, it is more mental abuse—*AND* with social media factored in, it can be much worse.

The scripture above says we should love our neighbor as ourselves. *"Neighbor"* refers to people. It is very hard to love someone who has been or who **IS** mean to you. Most of the time, when someone is a bully, that person is doing it to take attention off of themselves. They are very insecure and sensitive people. They don't love or even like themselves. They get a thrill out of mentally (and sometimes physically) abusing others. It makes them feel superior. It makes them feel good about themselves. In actuality, bullies have no courage at all!

Bullies have tormented some people so bad, the victim ends up committing suicide. Kids are scared to tell anyone because they don't want to be considered a tattle-tell or a snitch. Pay close attention to what I'm about to write next:

You only get **ONE** life. If someone is hurting you in *ANY* way, I give you permission to **TELL SOMEONE**. You may be threatened by the bully or abuser just to scare you. *TELL ANYWAY!*

The Bible commands us to love our neighbors as ourselves. Yes, that means even

Love Your Neighbor

those who are mean to you and unlovable. Yes, that means even people who pick on you and call you names. Yes, that means even those who make you feel inferior or 'less than'. **YES!** You are to love them, too.

Do you realize you do things that God doesn't approve of, yet He *STILL* loves you? It won't be easy loving someone who is mean to you — but it's necessary. Also, when people pick on you, it can cause **YOU** to feel bad about *YOU*. You begin to doubt and not like yourself. **DO NOT** allow anyone to have that much control over you. **REMEMBER**: You are fearfully and wonderfully made! You are more than a conqueror! You can do *ALL* things through Christ who gives you strength!

This topic also goes back to forgiveness. Just like God forgives you for **ANYTHING** that you do, you must also forgive those who hurt you. Again: It's *NOT* easy, but very necessary.

When people are mean and bullying you, it can cause you to become angry and bitter. Anger and bitterness cause sickness in your body. It begins to fester in you and you may suffer from headaches and stomachaches. You make yourself ***PHYSICALLY*** sick.

When people can cause you to act or feel a certain way, they have control over you. Again: Don't allow **ANYONE** to have that type of control over you.

Let's pause for a moment.

What if ***YOU*** are the one who is the bully? **STOP** right now. If someone is making you do it or you are being pressured to tease and pick on someone, you need to stop **RIGHT NOW**. If you are doing it to fit in with the crowd, **STOP**! Think

Love Your Neighbor

about *WHY* you would want to hurt or harm someone. Take a **GOOD** look at yourself and do some self-reflection. Imagine if it was your sister, brother, or other family member being bullied…

There is nothing you could be going through that should cause you to **WANT** to hurt someone else. Ask yourself "Why?" ***WHY*** are you causing harm to another? What if someone bullied you in the way you are doing another?

God wants us to **LOVE** and *NOT HURT* one another. It is important to treat others the way you want to be treated. If you are being bullied, **TELL SOMEONE**. If you *ARE* the bully, **STOP**. If you know someone being bullied, ***STAND UP FOR THEM.***

Eraina Tinnin

Personal Reflection

I wasn't bullied in school. I was, however, teased and picked on because of my name. **EVERYONE** had a problem pronouncing it correctly — students, teachers, doctors, and more. It made me not like my name while I was growing up *(as shared earlier)*.

I did have one experience in 7th grade in band class when a boy pulled the chair out from under me as I was going to sit down. Of course, I fell to the floor. I think a few people laughed but one girl actually went off on the boy. She told him he shouldn't have done that. I was embarrassed but I felt good knowing someone stood up for me.

I was very insecure and had low self-esteem growing up, so I didn't speak up for myself. That is why it impacted me in a powerful way when the girl in band class stood up for me.

Love Your Neighbor

I still remember her name. She probably wouldn't even remember the incident if I told her about it...

One thing I have **NEVER** done was tease or pick on someone. It hurts my heart when people are the target of bullying. The emotional and physical strain they go through has to hurt. Don't be the one to cause someone that kind of pain.

Eraina Tinnin

Affirmation

I will treat others the way
I want to be treated.

Love Your Neighbor

Activity

Write down ways that someone can be bullied. If you see someone being bullied, stand up for them and tell someone.

_____

_____

_____

_____

_____

_____

_____

_____

_____

_____

Chapter 9
Boys & Dating

"Do not be deceived: "Bad company corrupts good morals"".
1 Corinthians 15:33 (NIV)

When you are a teen (sometimes younger), you begin to think boys are 'cute'. There was a time in elementary school when you thought boys were yucky. ☺ Some time in middle school, your view changed and boys became 'cute'. That's where it all begins. Once you think a boy is 'cute', you never go back to thinking they are yucky.

Depending on your age, you may or may not be able to date. I already know one of the first things you will "like" about a boy is how he looks. It's human nature; it comes naturally. **BUT** there is so much more to dating than one's looks. Of course, that is what draws you in at first but there is so much more to dating. There are a few other things to look out for.

The first thing is to make sure he treats you right. When you first start dating, everything is peaches and cream—and then you get to know each other better. If he talks down to you, tries to control you, or belittles you, **RUN** (don't walk) away as fast as you can. If he tries to control all of your time or tries to make it seem like he is *SO* into you that he doesn't want to **SHARE** you or your time with family and friends, **RUN** as fast as you can. If he tries to control what you wear, how you style your hair, or tells you if you should wear makeup (depending, again, on your age), **RUN** as fast as you can.

DO NOT allow anyone to control you. You may think it is cute at first that a guy wants to spend *ALL* of his time with you — but it is **NOT** cute. If he talks to you disrespectfully in public **OR** private, **RUN** as fast as you can. Do not allow *ANYONE* to disrespect you.

You need to know what kind of guy you are interested in. Having a list of things could be a good thing...but it could also be a bad thing. A good thing is that it allows you to see what you desire in a boyfriend (and potential husband). Some people list physical attributes but keep in mind what you want physically may not be who **GOD** has for you. Keep in mind that someone who treats you like a ***QUEEN*** (yes, even as a teenager) is who you should be looking for; someone who doesn't disrespect your parents' rules, someone who doesn't talk to you any kind of way or try to control you, and someone who doesn't try to pressure you to do something you don't want to do (drugs, alcohol, sex, etc.). That guy should also have goals and dreams. Even a teenager should have dreams and something to work towards. After all, you aren't going to be a teen forever!

Even though dating and boys is part of the teen years, it should not be your main focus. Focus on your education. Focus on loving yourself. Focus on your goals and aspirations. Focus on being who God created you to be.

When you start dating, your focus begins to change. You start thinking about him: thinking about when you are going to see him again, what you are going to do, and the dates you are going to go on. With social media and today's technological advances, when you aren't together, you might text, face-time, Skype, direct message, and even tweet. It's important to not allow yourself to get distracted by boys because when you do, they become your priority. Boys aren't going anywhere. So, it is important at your age in life to keep the main thing the "main thing". The "main thing" would be school, your goals and future plans, having fun with your friends, and creating amazing memories.

Eraina Tinnin

Personal Reflection

I started having crushes on boys in middle school. I was the girl who, if I thought a boy was cute, he didn't like me in return. I had my first boyfriend my junior year of high school. He didn't have a car, so we really didn't see each other often because we went to different schools and didn't live near each other.

My senior year of high school, I had another boyfriend. We spent every day after school together **AND** most weekends. Our parents even met. Although we spent a lot of time together, I still made a point to spend time with my friends. I never got so lost in him that I forgot *ME*. I continued with my hobbies and interests. After graduating high school, I went off to college in another state. I did not allow my relationship to stop me from being *ME*.

Boys & Dating

If you do happen to date and end up with a boyfriend, be true to who you are. Don't allow anyone to change you, your vision, and your goals for yourself. Stay on the path to success.

Eraina Tinnin

Affirmation

I will make myself a priority.

Boys & Dating

Activity

Write down a list of things you enjoy doing. Make a point to do something you enjoy **EVERY** day.

_____

_____

_____

_____

_____

_____

_____

_____

_____

_____

Chapter 10
Just for Fun

"And whatever you do in word or deed, do all in the name of the Lord Jesus, giving thanks through Him to God the Father."
Colossians 3:17 (NIV)

What hobbies do you have? What do you enjoy doing? Everyone has things they enjoy doing outside of school, work, and hanging out with friends. You could be a creative arts person and like to sing, dance, write poetry, play an instrument, write stories, or paint. You may enjoy playing sports or video games, going to the movies, shopping, or reading. Your hobbies should be things that relax you and that you **ENJOY**.

Everyone may have different hobbies. Your friends may or may not have the same

Just for Fun

hobbies as you or your hobbies may be what brought you together. Life can get busy and you may begin to neglect your hobbies. It is important for you to always make time for things you enjoy doing. It is also important your hobbies are pleasing to God. You shouldn't have a hobby that consists of doing harm to you or someone else.

Your hobbies should also be things **YOU** enjoy doing. Often times, we may start doing something because our parents put us in it *(but we don't really **ENJOY** it)*. For instance, you may enjoy reading but your parents want you to play sports. If you have to play sports, make sure you are also doing something else you enjoy.

Your hobbies can be a way for you to relax after a tough day or a way to just have **FUN**! Whatever you do, make sure it's what *YOU* want to do. As you get older, life can get in the way of enjoying your hobbies. I often hear of adults who no longer do the things they once enjoyed because of their job, family life, or other responsibilities. Don't let that be you.

Just for Fun

Personal Reflection

My all-time favorite hobby is reading. My aunt taught me how to read when I was four years old. Growing up, you could always find me with my nose in a book.

I remember my grandparents telling me I need to go outside instead of reading so much. I did go outside and had fun but I much preferred being curled up with a good book. As an adult, I **ALWAYS** make time for reading. When I got married, had children, and a job, it was more difficult to find time to read — but I did it!

At one time, I was a Book-Reviewer and President of a local book club. I had the book club for 12 years. We went on trips together and enjoyed our monthly meetings. It was something I looked forward to each month. I no longer have the book club and I no longer review books but guess what? **I STILL READ.** I make sure I have a good book to read every day.

Just for Fun

Affirmation

I will always make time
for the things I ENJOY.

Activity

Make a list of things you enjoy doing and then **DO THEM** at least two to three times a week.

Just for Fun

Chapter 11
Parents Just Don't Understand

"Honor your father and mother, that your days may be prolonged in the land which the LORD your God gives you."
Exodus 20:12 (NIV)

The teen years can be a difficult time for you and your parents. You aren't really a child anymore. Well, you are a child; just not a little kid. 😊 You are starting to come into your own. You have your own interests and desires. You have your own goals and visions for yourself. You have your own personality, thoughts, and beliefs. As parents, it may be difficult seeing you transition from their "little baby" (although you will always be their little baby) into a teen and, eventually, an adult.

Parents Just Don't Understand

For some teens, this is a time when they grow more distant from their parents. They find it difficult to communicate, and parents find it difficult to communicate as well. It can be a very difficult time—but it doesn't **HAVE** to be.

I know people who couldn't *STAND* their parents during their teen years but can't imagine life without them as an adult. I also know people who have always had a good relationship with their parents and never had to deal with the difficulties typically associated with the teen transition years. You may think your parents don't understand you but keep this in mind: They were once teenagers, too.

The main thing to keep in mind is to openly communicate with your parents and keep them "in the know". I know this may be difficult because some parents aren't the "listening type" or because you simply may not have that type of relationship with them. I would encourage you to **TRY** to talk to them. Respect where they are coming from. Parents *WERE* once teenagers, so they do know some of the struggles you are dealing with. Granted it is a different time period now, although some things have changed, ***MOST*** have stayed the same.

Don't forget that your parents have your best interests at heart. So, when they say things that you may not agree with, like, or understand, know that they are looking out for **YOU**. They have 'been there' and can foresee problems that you may not see. On the other hand, parents also know that you learn from your *OWN* mistakes. They can't protect you from **EVERYTHING**, no matter how hard they try. This time in your life doesn't have to be difficult. Try to understand your parents' point of view. Hopefully, they will try to understand yours.

Parents Just Don't Understand

I stated earlier that although some things have changed, **MOST** have remained the same. Your parents were teenagers before and went through a lot of what you are currently going through. Don't underestimate them.

Personal Reflection

As a teenager, I had a pretty good relationship with my parents. I was a responsible child and could be trusted, so I never had a curfew. I didn't give in to peer pressure. I didn't smoke or drink. I enjoyed hanging out with my friends. We went to parties, movies, the mall, roller skating, etc.

One thing I think I like best about when I grew up was that there were no social media outlets or cell phones. We actually had great conversations and really got to know one another. I remember when I started dating, I would be on the phone for **HOURS**. My friends and I would talk for ***HOURS***. I had the nerve to get mad when one of my parents' friends called and interrupted MY call *(I didn't even pay a penny towards the bill)*.

Parents Just Don't Understand

I was fortunate to not have that awkward *"I hate my parents"* stage when I was a teen. There were things I chose not to tell them but that was a part of me growing into my own.

Since I am also a parent, I have raised two children who are now 21 and 22 years old. I am thanking God that we have an amazing relationship. They have **ALWAYS** talked to me about **EVERYTHING** *(and they still do)*. I never blew up or looked at them crazy. I listened and answered any questions they had—about **ANYTHING**. As adults, my children *STILL* trust me and share things with me. I thank God for our relationship. They know I will be there for them through thick and thin. They know they can talk to me and that I will always have their back. I will support, encourage, and inspire them.

I pray the same for you, your parents, and future children.

Eraina Tinnin

Affirmation

I will communicate honestly with my parents.

Parents Just Don't Understand

Activity

Make a date with your parents and **JUST TALK**. 😊 Journal the results. How did you feel?

_____

_____

_____

_____

_____

_____

_____

_____

_____

_____

_____

Eraina Tinnin

Chapter 12
Be Happy

"For his anger lasts only a moment, but his favor lasts a lifetime; weeping may stay for the night, but rejoicing comes in the morning."
Psalm 30:5 (NIV)

There will be times when you aren't happy. You may be sad. You may be angry. You may be depressed. You may be grieving. You may even be sick. No matter what you are going through, **JOY DOES COME IN THE MORNING!** The scripture above says so. 😊 Keep in mind this: Whatever you are going through in your life *WILL PASS*.

The teen years are a time of transition. You may not be sure of exactly **WHO** you are just yet. You will make some mistakes (we all did). You will do some things right and some things wrong (we all did). **DO NOT** allow it to change or turn you into someone you are not. Do not allow yourself to stay down for long. Jesus died on the cross and rose in ***THREE DAYS.*** Whenever you are going through something, do not allow it to keep you down more than *THREE DAYS*.

You deserve to be happy. One thing I want you to keep in mind is that this is **YOUR** life. You only get *ONE* chance and *ONE* life. People will try to tell you what to do or convince you to do what's best for **YOUR LIFE.**

One of my favorite scriptures is Jeremiah 29:11:

"For I know the plans I have for you", declares the Lord; "Plans to prosper you and not harm you, plans to give you a hope and future."

God has plans for you. Even you being born was in God's plan. You are here for a reason

Be Happy

AND have a purpose. You should live your life happily and full of *JOY*. People will try to come and steal your joy. Although you can't control that, you **CAN** control *YOU* (your reaction and response).

You will encounter people who try to bring you down. People may talk bad about you and even lie on you. Through it all, you need to protect your peace and your happiness. Do not allow anyone to change your attitude or steal your joy. **GOD** gave it to you; don't allow anyone to take it away!

At some point, you will no longer be a teenager. You will graduate high school and go off to college, the military, or whatever you choose to do. Keep in mind: This is **YOUR** life. God gave you a gift. We *ALL* have them. Use the gifts God gave you.

Eraina Tinnin

Often times, adults forget the dreams they had when they were younger. Don't let your dreams die. There are so many dreams buried in cemeteries. Don't let yours be one of them.

Be Happy

Personal Reflection

For the most part, I am happy. People have called me "Sunshine", a "Ray of Sun Bubbles", and "Giggles" — just to name a few. I always try to bring light to those around me.

There was a time when I suffered from depression, fear, and had low self-esteem. I also cared what people thought about me. All of the things named **DO NOT** bring happiness. It wasn't until I began to read the Word of God, apply the Word of God, and develop a relationship with God that I no longer suffered from those things.

I am now in a much happier place. I am no longer trying to please people. I am no longer afraid to say "no". I am no longer living my life for everyone else. I am doing what I believe God called me to be and do, with *WRITING* being one of those things.

Make sure you make the most of your life. You only get **ONE**.

Be Happy

Affirmation

I will not allow anyone nor anything to steal my joy.

Eraina Tinnin

Activity

Write down a list of things that you enjoy doing that make you happy. Make a promise to yourself to always **MAKE TIME** to do those things for the *REST* of your life.

_____

_____

_____

_____

_____

_____

_____

_____

_____

_____

Be Happy

Chapter 13
Social Media

*"Making the best use of the time,
because the days are evil."*
Ephesians 5:6 (ESV)

Social media is **EVERYTHING** in this day and age. So much of life is on Facebook, Instagram, Twitter, Snapchat, YouTube, and more. Although social media can be used for good, it can also be used for bad.

I have found with social media, relationships are not being developed. There is not much talking. There is not much hanging out. There is not much going to the movies. There is not much dating. There is not much family time. When those things are done, the *CELL PHONE* is right in the center occupying one's time.

Social media can be used for good. People share events, meet new people, raise funds for a

Social Media

good cause, share accomplishments and pictures of the family, and so much more. I am all for this type of sharing.

Social media is only as bad as the person posting makes it. It has been used to cyber-bully people, which in turn has caused some to end their life due to the embarrassment and humiliation. It has been used to lie on people others may not like. People have used it to fight back and forth. It has also been used to help. If something happened and no one was sure *WHAT* exactly happened, you can rest assured **SOMEONE** has recorded it *(that could be a good thing)*.

Social media has also been used for people to pretend they are someone else. They create fake profiles with a fake picture and, basically, a fake life. They trick people into friending them and even sometimes dating them and falling in love *(called 'Catfish')*. It is sad that people feel they have to do that.

Social media has been used to make people famous—some in a good way; others in a bad one. A post can go "viral" in a matter of seconds and make someone's life great…or ruin it.

Social media is even used to make money and build businesses. It has even been used to pay tribute to a loved one who may have passed away. It's also a way to keep in touch with friends and family that live far away. Companies and schools even look at potential employees' and students' profiles to see if they will hire or accept them into their school.

As you can see, there are a **LOT** of uses for social media; some good, some not so good. One thing I want you to keep in mind in this era of social media is to always "*be who you **POST** to be*". Don't post things that are untrue by trying to be

Social Media

someone you are not while concerning yourself with the 'likes' and 'shares'. Use it for good and not to gossip or spread rumors about others.

Also, **PLEASE** keep in mind that *WHATEVER* you post on the internet will be there **FOREVER**. So, make sure you make smart choices.

Imagine posting something on the internet at the age you are now and later seeing it as an adult with children. Would you want your future children to **SEE** what you have posted? Would you want a potential employer or college to see what you have posted?

Keep in mind: What you post is there…**FOREVER**—even if you hit that 'delete' button!

Eraina Tinnin

Personal Reflection

As mentioned previously, one thing I am glad about is that we **DID NOT** have social media when I was growing up. As a child, I enjoyed spending time outside playing games, riding bikes, and just having fun. As a teenager, I loved hanging out with my friends going to the movies, the mall, skating, parties, or just hanging out at each other's house. Spending hours and hours talking on the phone was one of the highlights of my teen years. Looking back, I have *NO* idea what we talked about for so long but you can best believe that we **REALLY** knew each other and developed some really great, meaningful friendships.

In college, we would hang out on the yard (campus) into the wee hours of the morning just talking and having fun. We didn't have to worry about something being posted or recorded. We

Social Media

had no concerns about 'likes' or 'shares' because social media didn't exist.

As an adult, I use social media to inspire and encourage. I also use it to build my business online and keep in touch with family and friends. It is great to use—if used in a **POSITIVE** way.

Eraina Tinnin

Affirmation

I will use social media for good and not bad.

Social Media

Activity

See how long you can go **WITHOUT** posting on social media. Take the time to, instead, do something else you enjoy (reading, drawing, singing, dancing, etc.). Write down how you felt after stepping away from social media and indulged in that other activity.

_____

_____

_____

_____

_____

_____

_____

_____

Eraina Tinnin

You Are a Gift

Words of Encouragement

When my three daughters were younger, I taught them this affirmation: "I am a child of God and I am beautiful, strong, intelligent, talented, and wonderful. I seek the beauty, strength, intelligence, talent, and wonder in everyone else. I am of African descent and I am proud of my heritage." We'd say it aloud daily. In addition, I'd ask them to tell at least three things for which they were grateful. When life's inevitable challenges show up, I want my daughters to have a firm foundation rooted in faith, self-confidence, a positive outlook, and gratitude. I want this for all of you, too—especially as you navigate the uniquely challenging years of middle school and high school.

~ Christine L. ~

****

You are fabulous and you are special to God. You'll experience so many things on this journey; some will be joyous and some will be painful but your constant is the LOVE of God. He loves you so much and has created you with your own unique beauty, style, intelligence, personality, and spirit. Stay close to Him through His Word and prayer, and watch Him work.

~ Stacy M. ~

****

I know it is not easy growing as a young lady who will turn into a woman. You are trying to figure out who you are. I want you to always remember this: "Every good and perfect gift is from above" (James 1:17). You are a gift from God to the world. Never let anyone treat you or tell you any different. Love yourself first and others will love you in return.

~ Cheryl P. ~

Words from the Author

God gave me the vision for this book. In life, there are **MANY** ups and downs and **MANY** uncertainties. You might not know what's going to happen from one minute to the next—and that's okay. That's when you rely on God to guide you. You may not be able to control other people and what happens to you but you can control *YOUR* actions, *YOUR* words, and *YOUR* thoughts. Remember that.

The most important thing I want you to take away from this book is that **YOU ARE A GIFT**. You are precious and should be treated as such. You should be treated as a gift—not just by yourself but other people as well. During everything that happens to you, ***REMEMBER THAT.***

When you have decisions to make, when people talk to you certain ways, or when they treat you a certain way, ask yourself if you are being treated like the **QUEEN** you are. You *ARE* a **QUEEN**! All of the topics discussed in this book are areas where you can show your **'QUEENDOM'**!

Another of my favorite scriptures in the Bible is 1st Peter 2:9. It says:

*"But you are a chosen people, a royal priesthood, a holy nation, **<u>God's special possession</u>**, that you may declare the praises of Him who called you out of darkness into His wonderful light."*

That scripture tells me that I am **SPECIAL** — and **you** are, too!

This book is based off of the scripture Psalm 127:3 which says, "***<u>Children are a gift</u>*** *from the LORD; they are a reward from Him*". If **GOD** says you are a gift and a reward, that's *ALL* you need to know. It doesn't matter what anyone else says, thinks, or does. **GOD SAYS** you are a **GIFT**!

You Are a Gift

Stop right now and repeat the following words aloud until you **BELIEVE** them: **GOD SAYS I AM A GIFT. GOD SAYS I AM A GIFT. GOD SAYS I AM A GIFT.**

Believe it. Believe it in *EVERYTHING* you do and *EVERYTHING* you say.

I pray this book has been a blessing to you. I pray it helps you think about things you may not have thought about before. I pray it helps you grow into the **QUEEN** you are destined to be.

I would love to hear your thoughts on this book. Please feel free to send me an email letting me know!

Eraina.Tinnin@gmail.com

Eraina Tinnin

About the Author

Eraina Tinnin is an Inspirational Speaker, Empowerment Coach, International Best-Selling Author, Self-Love Strategist, and Entrepreneur. She has been named an "Encourager" because of her unfailing ability to lift the spirits of others and is affectionately known as the 'Inspirational Powerhouse'.

Eraina is the Founder of Eraina Tinnin Unlimited **and** 'Sistahs in Spirit'—an online ministry. She is a Contributing Writer with *Authentically You Magazine*; Author of *Becoming a Beautiful You 100-Day Devotional*; Co-Host of Beautiful You Authentic You Radio Show; and Co-Founder of Beautiful You Authentic You. To her credit, she is also a Co-Author of the following Best-Selling Titles:

- *Healing Toxic Habits*
- *Affirmations & Antidotes That Remind Me*
- *The Woman Behind the Mask: Identifying the Woman Hidden*

Eraina has a Master's Degree in Human Services with a specialization in Marriage & Family Therapy. She resides in North Carolina with her husband, Corey, and has two adult children.

Connect with Eraina Tinnin:

Web: www.ErainaTinninUnlimited.com

Email: Eraina.Tinnin@gmail.com

Instagram: Eraina_BeautifullyBecoming

Phone: 1-800-430-5436

Mail: P.O. Box 38901
 Greensboro, NC 27438

www.ingramcontent.com/pod-product-compliance
Lightning Source LLC
Chambersburg PA
CBHW070108120526
44588CB00032B/1385